Sylvia Gainsford NDD (BA) ATD, has been a professional artist since 1974. She has exhibited at the Royal Academy and her paintings have sold in Europe and the United States, including work commissioned for a Beverly Hills foundation. Buckingham Fine Art Publishers and The Medici Society have reproduced her paintings and, in addition to private sales, she creates a variety of illustration work for London publishers.

Sylvia and her artist husband Leon Olin had their first book, *Food from the Countryside*, published in 1989, and have their own 'Gallery One' in Fishguard, Wales.

Author **Howard Rodway** has been involved in the occult world for over thirty-five years. During this time he has been public relations manager for the late psychic Kim Tracey and also for Dr Francis Ngombe, President of the Association of African and Asian Medicine Men.

Howard's first book *The Psychic Directory* was published in 1984. He wrote a series of articles about the occult for London's *Metropolitan* magazine in the mid eighties, and also had a short story published.

Sylvia Gainsford and **Howard Rodway** have worked together on a number of projects, including most notably *Tarot of Northern Shadows* (1998) and *Tarot of the Old Path* (1990). Their work is well known and the Atlantic, with *Tarot of the* selling card decks in the US.

GW00645072

THE ARTIST'S DEDICATION

To my husband Leon Olin – a fellow professional artist
and inspiration for my runic images.

To Norah Louise Gainsford – your prayer was answered.

To Lee Davies – who made me my first rune stones and advised on
Norse mythology for Tarot of Northern Shadows.

To Pat Gillespie – an inspirational friendship.

To Raymond Lewis for his reference photographs of Norway.

To Kes Enright – a gifted seer.

THE AUTHOR'S DEDICATION AND ACKNOWLEDGEMENTS

To Kim Tracey – who has a special place in the contemporary
history of the runes. Remembered with affection and respect.

To our editor Susan Lascelles for her enthusiastic
response to this project.

To Paul Tidmarsh for his card diagram
computer graphics.

And to my wife Marie for her critical comment
and editing skill.

RAIDO
The god Thor

TEIWAZ
The god Tiu

URUZ
The god Vidar

DAGAZ
The goddess Verdandi

THE
RUNE
VISION
CARDS

Sylvia Gainsford with Howard Rodway

vega

© Vega 2002
Card illustrations © Sylvia Gainsford 2002
Text © Howard Rodway 2002

First published in the UK in 2001 by Vega
8-10 Blenheim Court, Brewery Road, London, N7 9NY

A member of **Chrysalis** Books plc

Cover illustration by Sylvia Gainsford
Designed and typeset by Becky Willis, Design Revolution, Brighton
Text illustrations by Sylvia Gainsford
Diagram Graphics by Paul Tidmarsh
Printed and bound in China

British Library Cataloguing in Publication data available

ISBN 1 84333 023 7

Contents

Song of Odin

I know that I hung on that windy tree,
Spear-wounded, nine full nights,
Given to Odin, myself to myself,
On that tree that rose from roots
That no man knows.

They gave me neither bread nor drink from horn,
I peered below.
I clutched the runes, screaming I grabbed them,
And then sank back.

I had nine mighty songs from that famed
Son of Bölthor, father of Bestla,

And one swig I snatched of that glorious mead
Drained from Ódrerir.

Then quickened and flourished
Sprouted and throve.
From a single word, another sprung:
From a single deed, another sprung.

From the Icelandic *Poetic Edda* (circa 1270–80)

Author's Note

I was very fortunate as a child to have had a mother who had, and has, second sight, so from an early age I regarded it as quite normal that the future could be foretold. Growing up in such an environment made it quite natural for me later in life to mix and associate with spiritualists, witches and psychics. I learned from them all, but it was not until my wife Marie and I moved to the south-east of England in the mid seventies that I heard of the runes for the first time.

An acquaintance in Kent told me about a psychic by the name of Kim Tracey who used 'runes' when she gave private readings. 'What on earth are runes?' I asked.

The only way to satisfy my curiosity was to make an appointment to have a reading with this psychic. I did just that and within a couple of weeks I was sitting before Kim Tracey with twenty-five little domino-shaped blocks on the table between us. The 'stones', as she referred to them, had unusual symbols carved upon their faces. I had never seen anything like them before.

Kim started the reading by asking me to turn the runes face down, shuffle them and then place the stones in twos to form a circle. The reading that she gave me, as she turned over each pair of stones and concentrated on their meanings, was a revelation in more than one sense of the word. She read the runes with confident, precise detail and without hesitation. It was obvious that she was very gifted because she touched on details from my past and present that were uncannily correct. Time would tell though whether her predictions for the future were just as accurate ... and it turned out that they were! It was obvious that the runes were a unique and precise form of divination, especially when used by a gifted psychic. I was impressed!

I kept in touch with Kim Tracey and just before the 1978 publication of her autobiography *Secrets of the Runes*, Kim asked me to look after public relations for her. I accepted her invitation and that was the start of another interesting period in my life because, from knowing nothing at all about the runes, I acquired inside knowledge about these ancient symbols from the very person responsible for bringing them into the public spotlight.

Only hours after I finished writing the above paragraph, I received a telephone call from Kim's daughter Dallas. She told me that her mother had passed away during the evening before. This story therefore is my tribute to Kim Tracey.

Howard Rodway

Foreword

Around two thousand years ago in northern Europe, a set of letters was created by the Germanic peoples, which they named 'runes', from the Gothic *runa* meaning 'secret' or 'a mystery'. These letters were indeed a mystery because they encompassed long-established traditions and beliefs, from the most sacred religious aspects to the everyday mundane activities. Hence, their power as a tool for divination was undoubtedly magical.

Widely used in the ancient world, the runic oracle served a ritual function to evoke the puissant influence of the Norse gods and goddesses that it represented. Therefore, the craft of the rune masters and mistresses included runes and spells to affect the weather, crops, healing and love; runes for fertility, taking off curses, attracting good luck and gaining protection.

A large number of runic practitioners were female and an excellent description of a thirteenth-century mistress of runecraft, by the unknown author, occurs in the Saga of Erik the Red: "She wore a cloak set with stones along the hem. Around her neck and covering her head she wore a hood lined with white catskins. In one hand she carried a staff with a knob on the end and at her belt, holding together her long dress, hung a charm pouch."

In recent times, the Scandinavian runes have received less attention than other forms of divination. However, in her brilliantly executed Rune Vision Cards, artist Sylvia Gainsford has created an exciting new concept for these ancient, magical letters and combined them with the timeless spirit forms of the Norse deities, together with their appropriate symbols and meanings.

These cards vividly portray the runes, some of which feature actual landscapes in Norway. They also include atavistic animals and birds associated with each god and goddess, depicted in the artist's usual masterly style.

Howard Rodway's incisive commentary on this fresh approach to the runes will provide a valuable aid, whether the runes are utilized for divination, meditation or to become *en rapport* with the Norse deities and traditions.

Patricia C Crowther

Introduction

Norse mythology associates the runes with the one-eyed Norse god Odin who, to acquire knowledge of this mystical alphabet, hung from the giant ash tree Yggdrasil for nine days and nights impaled on his own spear.

The magical knowledge of the runes was used by magicians and shamans for the purposes of prophecy, counselling, healing, spell-working, fertility rites and to gain victory in battle. The symbols were also engraved on jewellery and armour to provide protection. Perhaps surprisingly, comparatively little use was made of the runic alphabet as an ordinary means of communication.

Examples of old runic inscriptions can be found today north of Stavanger in Norway, Bjolderup in Sweden, Maes Howe in the Orkney Islands and in numerous museums around the world, including Oslo's University Museum.

At the present time the runes are again being used for prediction, counselling, healing, spell-working and for engraving on jewellery. Today, as in the recent past, some rune signs are also used as political symbols. The Campaign for Nuclear Disarmament is identified with the rune Algiz, the Scottish Nationalist Party has adopted the rune Othila as the SNP badge, and double Sowulo (or Sigil) runes were used as the emblem for Heinrich Himmler's infamous SS (Schutzstaffel) during the Nazi (Nationalsozialist) era in Germany during the

1930s and 1940s. The latter example is a warning that magical tools can be used for a negative as well as a positive purpose.

There are several mystical alphabets that are currently used by occultists and witches but it is the runes that have really gained favour since the late 1970s. In my opinion, one person is responsible for this, the late psychic and writer Kim Tracey who passed on in September 1999. This skilled seer started giving rune readings in the mid-seventies and then brought the ancient symbols to public attention in her autobiography, *Secrets of the Runes.*

Rune Vision Cards creator-artist Sylvia Gainsford is another such gifted person. Sylvia received enormous praise for her beautiful *Tarot of the Old Path*, a set of cards first produced in 1990, the popularity of which ensured the success of Sylvia's *Tarot of Northern Shadows*, which followed in 1998. In *Northern Shadows* she introduces the runes to good effect to emphasize the theme of this particular Tarot.

It was destined that Sylvia Gainsford's interest in runic lore would inevitably lead her to produce her own rune cards, and so it was that the Rune Vision Cards materialized. Sylvia's images in these cards project such a magical dimension that it is quite obvious that she is finely attuned to the mystical realm.

In the Rune Vision Cards, the runes, rather than being mere signs or symbols, are immediately taken to a different dimension when set against Sylvia's beautiful pictures. This artist's outstanding illustrations provide a particularly sensitive psychic focus that will, I am sure, transport you to a different level of consciousness.

In this book you will find descriptive text for each of Sylvia's Rune Vision Cards together with divinatory meanings and rune correspondences (associated symbols). Also included are descriptions of three different card layouts, with diagrams.

Sylvia and I wish you many magical and mystical moments with the Rune Vision Cards.

The Runic Alphabet

The Norse runes are divided into three distinct groups, also called aetts. These groups are:

Numbers 1–8 belonging to the goddess Freya/Frejya
Numbers 9–16 belonging to the god Hagal
Numbers 17–24 belonging to the god Týr
The blank rune number 25 exists on its own.

Note: There are nine runes that look the same whether in the upright or reversed position. These particular symbols do not normally have reverse meanings. The Rune Vision Cards however make an exception to the rule because these nine signs are contained within Sylvia Gainsford's visual images which, when reversed, are obviously upside down. As a point of reference, and for your information, these nine cards have their reversed meanings sections marked with an asterisk. The blank rune, with its one set of meanings, has neither an upright or reversed position.

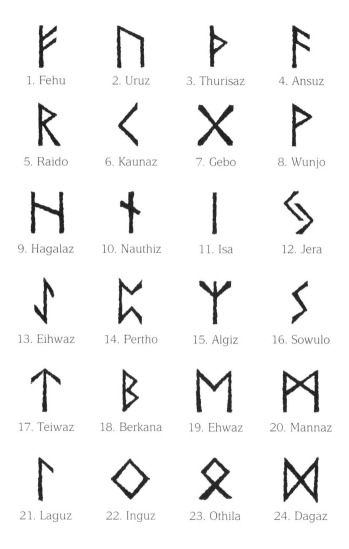

1. Fehu
2. Uruz
3. Thurisaz
4. Ansuz
5. Raido
6. Kaunaz
7. Gebo
8. Wunjo
9. Hagalaz
10. Nauthiz
11. Isa
12. Jera
13. Eihwaz
14. Pertho
15. Algiz
16. Sowulo
17. Teiwaz
18. Berkana
19. Ehwaz
20. Mannaz
21. Laguz
22. Inguz
23. Othila
24. Dagaz

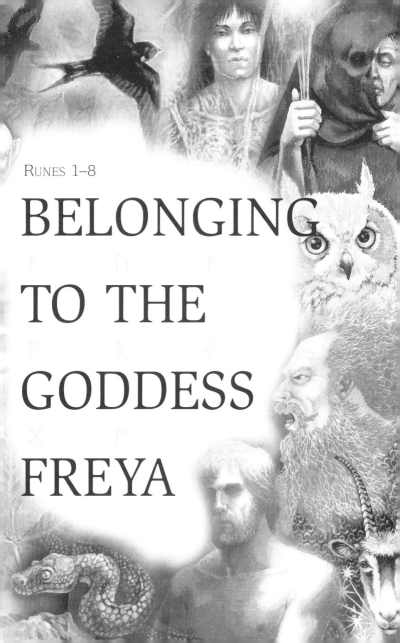

BELONGING TO THE GODDESS FREYA

1 Fehu

The goddess Freya
Meaning of symbol: Cattle

The goddess Freya is depicted with her falcon wings. The feathers grow from her arms, held forward to protect yet reveal her nude feminine form. Freya embodies the sensuality of the lover and mistress, whereas Frigg (card number 14) represents the good wife and mother.

Decorating Freya's neck and breast is a gold necklace, an emblem of the stars and the fecundity of the earth.

Freya hovers in flight in a sky of soft clouds in which a swallow flies high in the foreground. Beneath the goddess's wings is a sprig and flower of the elder, Fehu's tree.

Emerging from the clouds is the profile of a grey tabby cat's head, white whiskers spread forward, its bright-yellow eye gazing ahead. Grey cats are always associated with Freya.

At the top right-hand corner of this scene is the rune Fehu which is shown in red, the correct colour for this symbol.

The Goddess Freya (or Freyja)

The goddess Freya was an initiated high priestess and her brother Freyr was made a high priest. She was the offspring of Njörd the sea god, the controller of wind, tides and fire, and the guardian of seafarers and ships.

Freya was beautiful, with fair hair and blue eyes. She married Odur, the symbol of the summer sun, passion and love. When she was parted from Odur, Freya is said to have travelled the world searching for him, weeping as she went. Her tears trickled down into the ground and turned into gold. This metal is the basis of humanity's wealth, and wealth is the image of this rune.

Freya's liaisons were numerous and she was quite capable of fulfilling her desires by exploiting her sexual attractions. To gain her most valued possession, the brightly shining necklace called Brisingamen, she granted sexual favours to the four dwarves of Svartálfaheim.

Freya was the goddess of love, war, witchcraft, beauty and fruitfulness. Her chariot was drawn by grey cats, her favourite animals.

FEHU'S SYMBOLS
Meaning: Cattle
Image: Wealth
Object: Necklace
Animal: Cat and swallow
Goddess: Freya
Tree: Elder
Colour: Red

DIVINATORY SIGNIFICANCE
Financial strength and prosperity is close.
Love fulfilled. Desires nourished.

REVERSED
Love thwarted. Disappointment. A quarrel.
Possible financial worries.

ᚢ

2 Uruz

The god Vidar
Meaning of symbol: Aurochs

Vidar, the god associated with Uruz, is seen as a tree spirit. He merges with gnarled tree forms as he sits cross-legged, his left hand raised with the index finger extended in an attitude of authority and wisdom. His expression is that of one lost in thought. On Vidar's right foot is a thick leather and segmented iron shoe. The formation of the gnarled bark of the ancient tree becomes part of his torso and his feet rest by the roots. Other trees are seen in the forest, and the head of an aurochs, the animal identified with this rune, is visible between the branches. The aurochs, now extinct, was a wild ox that, once tamed, could be harnessed to work in the fields. These animals were also a valued source of meat and hide. The image of 'achievement' is expressed by the ability of man to tame and use these beasts.

Traditionally, Vidar dwelt within an impenetrable forest and the hall of his woodland home was decorated with wild flowers, so around him can be seen bluebells, primroses and ramsons, with the white flowers of bindweed trailing across his bare foot.

The sign of Uruz is in the lower left-hand corner. Uruz is shown in purple, the colour associated with this rune.

The God Vidar

Vidar, the son of Odin and Grid the giantess, was reclusive, wise and strong. His physical strength was considered to be almost equal to that of the mighty Thor, so he was a force to be reckoned with and a deity to be treated with respect. Vidar's attributes would be decisive on the day of the final conflict between good and evil.

Vidar lived in quiet solitude in his forest palace. He was usually clad in armour and armed with a broad-bladed sword.

The main feature of this god's apparel was the thick leather and segmented iron shoe that he wore on his right foot (right representing the physical side of the brain). This shoe was destined to be used on the last day of the world, which would be destroyed by fire. Vidar, with his strength, speed and quick reactions, would be victorious against Fenris Wolf. This conflict would end in total devastation, but Vidar would survive to rule in a new world.

Uruz is a rune with a strong emphasis on endings and beginnings, and these divinatory interpretations can be symbolized by the final conflict from which a new world will emerge.

If you draw this rune you should be prepared for change and progress.

URUZ'S SYMBOLS

Meaning: Aurochs

Image: Achievement

Object: Shoe

Animal: Aurochs

God: Vidar

Tree: None

Colour: Purple

DIVINATORY SIGNIFICANCE

Strength. Well-being. Support or news from afar.
Be alert to an opportunity.

REVERSED

Powers at a low ebb. A lost opportunity.

ᚦ

3 Thurisaz

The god Loki

Meaning of symbol: Giant

A snow-covered mountainous landscape is seen beyond the icebergs and rippling water of the foreground. The snow on the mountains reflects a warm tinge of light from an unseen sun, in contrast to the dark brooding sky. The distant high peak is Hornsundtind in Norway.

The vast shadowy figure is the god Loki who, although kneeling, towers into the clouds. Loki's eyes are lost in shadow. His strong arms and hands are tense and his fingers dip into the icy water. Above his left shoulder hangs the purple-hued rune Thurisaz. Opposite is a symbolic knife, its tip catching the light. This object, which can be either a useful tool or a lethal weapon, expresses Loki's mercurial temperament.

Looming forward from behind Loki is a snake, the symbol of magical containment and the power of the unconscious. According to Norse legend, Loki fathered the mighty snake Jörmungand, which encircled the middle world of Midgard.

In the lower right foreground can be seen a sprig of blackthorn, a plant associated with Thurisaz, thus completing the imagery for this rune.

The God Loki

The old god Loki has ancient roots, and some theorists, including artist Sylvia Gainsford, take him back to the stone age. But, whatever form he took as the deity of the hearth fire, he had a place of great importance in the hierarchy of the gods due to man's realization that fire could be controlled for protection, warmth and cooking.

Loki, a member of the Aesir, a group of important gods and goddesses who lived in Ásgard, was known as the Prince of Lies and the Sly One, and he delighted in causing mischief and mayhem with his pranks. He was a trickster who shape-shifted, using his magical ability for personal gain. Loki's personality was the exact opposite of Odin, his blood brother. Loki degenerated from making mischief to selfish malevolence and he was destined, because of the death of Baldur the solar god, to be responsible for triggering Ragnarök, the final conflict that resulted in the destruction of the world.

The possibility of change is one of the divinatory meanings expressed in this rune. Loki's character traits of mischief making and unreliability are also elements that are expressed through this rune.

THURISAZ'S SYMBOLS

Meaning: Giant
Image: Mercurial
Object: Knife
Animal: Snake
God: Loki
Tree: Blackthorn
Colour: Purple

DIVINATORY SIGNIFICANCE

Mischief making. Unreliability. A possible change. Do not act in haste because time will reveal a solution.

REVERSED

A hasty decision causes anxiety and regret.

ᚠ

4 Ansuz

The god Odin

Meaning of symbol: God

The blue-hooded head of the god Odin is seen half in shadow, with one eye gazing forward. Odin's expression is benign, his beard is greying and he is smiling slightly. To one side of him is one of his two wolves, Geri and Freki (the greedy ones). The wolf looks ahead, alert, on guard and watchful.

Odin is wrapped in his cloak, which symbolizes the sky through whose clouds two ravens fly. These pet birds, who acted as observers for their master, are named Huginn (thought) and Muninn (memory).

The spear Gungnir, its name inscribed in runic characters, rises on the left. A sprig of ash, expressing the importance of the mighty ash tree Yggdrasil that linked the three worlds via its roots, is at the bottom of the picture. Ash is also the tree from which the first man was made.

In the lower right-hand corner the sign of Ansuz is shown in purple, this rune's governing colour.

The God Odin

Odin, also known as the All-Father, was the most revered and highest of all the gods and the one who was recognized as their most powerful leader.

To be blessed by Odin was the greatest honour for gods and men alike. The early Nordic warrior went into battle secure in the knowledge that, should he be slain, a life in the halls of Valhalla in the company of the All-Father awaited him.

Traditionally, Odin is depicted wearing a blue hood and a blue-grey, cloud-flecked cloak symbolizing the sky. His throne Hlidskiálf was at the highest vantage point in Asgard, the realm of the gods. His companions were the two ravens Huginn and Muninn and the two wolves, Geri and Freki, that he fed by hand from food offered in worship to this god.

The most popular legend about Odin is of course the story of how, in order to gain the secrets of the runes and the wisdom of the dead, he performed an act of self-sacrifice by hanging from the ash tree Yggdrasil for nine days and nights impaled on his own spear.

One of the divinatory meanings of this rune is contact with an older person. This element is reflected in the family relationships that Odin enjoyed.

ANSUZ'S SYMBOLS

Meaning: God

Image: Blessing

Object: Spear

Animal: Wolf

God: Odin

Tree: Ash

Colour: Purple

DIVINATORY SIGNIFICANCE

A visit, gift or advice from an older person.
Learning wisdom.

REVERSED

Interference from an older person. Duplicity.

5 Raido

The god Thor
Meaning of symbol: Thunder

The mighty god Thor is seen here against the background of a thunderous sky, shouting ferociously, his windswept, flaming red hair and beard accentuating his strong, rugged face. Held to his chest in an iron-gauntlet-clad hand is his hammer Mjöllnir, which symbolizes male fertility. Streaks of lightning flash from the implement. The meaning of Raido is thunder, in the form of uncontrollable energy.

In the foreground is the head of a goat. The creature gazes at the onlooker and sparks fly from its mouth. Thor's chariot was drawn by goats, the animal associated with Raido. Below Thor's hammer is a sprig of oak with an acorn. The oak, standing for strength and bravery, is identified with this rune.

At the top left-hand corner the sign for Raido is shown in blue, the colour correspondence of this symbol.

The God Thor

Thor, the god associated with the rune Raido, was the son of Odin and Jörd. He was a fertility figure and the patron god of farmers and peasants. His mighty hammer Mjöllnir represented the power of male fertility and the regeneration of life in the earth.

Thor had a fiery temper that was quickly aroused. In contrast to his violent capabilities he also had a soft heart. He was the protector of the working person and was probably worshipped more widely than was Odin.

The familiar image of Thor depicts him in his chariot drawn by two goats. His journeys between Asgard and Midgard were made that much longer because he was forbidden to traverse the rainbow Bifrost for fear that he might damage the bridge with his weight and lightning flashes.

A journey and a travelling lifestyle are possible interpretations with this rune and these elements are symbolized by Thor's travels. 'Making a decision' is of divinatory significance with Raido too and this interpretation is symbolized by Thor's reaction to any given situation. He could be good-humoured or he could react with a swift and violent temper. The decision he made on how to react was a decision on how to communicate his feelings, and communication also has significance with this rune.

When Christianity replaced paganism, Thor was transformed into St Nicholas.

RAIDO'S SYMBOLS

Meaning: Thunder

Image: Journey

Object: Hammer

Animal: Goat

God: Thor

Tree: Oak

Colour: Blue

DIVINATORY SIGNIFICANCE

A journey. Travel for relaxation and pleasure.
A decision made to achieve an ambition.
Career prospects. Communication.

REVERSED

Arrangements hampered by a journey.
Plans obstructed. A lack of direction.

<

6 Kaunaz

The goddess Skuld

Meaning of symbol: Discomfort

The cloaked form of Skuld is traditionally shown with her face partly hidden. Her left hand clasps the cloak's hood to half cover her pained expression. Within the folds of the hood there can be seen the form of a skull. This indicates Skuld's knowledge of the future. In the goddess's right hand is a flaming torch, the object associated with this rune. The smoke from the torch forms dark clouds in the sky. A torch can have dual significance; it can be seen to express enlightenment (with which Skuld is identified) and to express Skuld shedding light on the future.

In the foreground to the left is the head of an owl, the bird identified with Kaunaz and traditionally regarded as a symbol both of wisdom and death. The owl portrayed here is a short-eared owl with characteristic orange eyes. A pine cone and leaves of the arolla pine, a common conifer in northern Europe, are shown too. The pine tree is Kaunaz's tree.

In the top right corner is the symbol for Kaunaz, which is shown in this rune's colour correspondence of blue.

The Goddess Skuld

Skuld was one of the three Norn sisters whose mission in life was to impart wisdom to the gods. This goddess is therefore identified with enlightenment, which is one of the divinatory meanings of this rune. The other two sisters, Urd and Verdandi, represented the past and present. They were able to warn the gods of evil to come and could point out a wise course of action in the present. The past was valuable too because lessons could be learnt from experience.

The three goddesses were wise and knowledgeable females who directed the fate of man. The gods visited and consulted the sisters and Odin also sought their advice, but the ultimate fate of the gods was kept secret by these three.

The Norns lived near the Urdar Fountain, from which Skuld would collect water for the roots of the sacred ash tree Yggdrasil. She would also put fresh earth around the tree's roots. Skuld's concern for the health of the tree reflects the significance of health matters with this rune.

Apart from her other activities, Skuld rode with the Valkyries to collect those warriors slain on the field of battle. This goddess is therefore associated with adverse conditions that are linked to Kaunaz.

KAUNAZ'S SYMBOLS

Meaning: Discomfort

Image: Illness

Object: Torch

Animal: Owl

Goddess: Skuld

Tree: Pine

Colour: Blue

DIVINATORY SIGNIFICANCE

For a woman, good fortune. A gift from a man.
For a man, pleasure from giving. Lust. Empathy.
Enlightenment. The possibility of health problems.
Physical or mental discomfort.

REVERSED

Loss. Ending. Resignation. Facing the inevitable.
Casting out the things of the past.

7 Gebo

The goddess Gefjon
Meaning of symbol: Gift

The maidenly and slim figure of the seated goddess Gefjon fills the sky above the mountains near Reine in Lofoten, Norway. Her face is shown in profile as she gazes into the crystal ball which she holds in her left hand. Gefjon's nude form is illuminated by the light from the crystal. Gebo's object is glass or crystal, which expresses light and purity, linking with Gefjon who was endowed with virginal qualities and protected all pure maidens.

An ox, the symbolic animal, for this rune, stands in the foreground. The ox expresses strength and patience, and is another link with Gefjon, who turned her sons into oxen.

At the top right of this scene is the symbol for Gebo which is shown in its associated colour of blue.

The Goddess Gefjon

Gefjon, the deity associated with Gebo, was the goddess of unwed women. She dwelt in Frigg's palace where she welcomed these females when they died. They were made comfortable there and would be happy forever after under Gefjon's protection.

Gefjon also has a close association with ploughing. Legend records that she had four sons by one of the giants. These four she changed into oxen so that she could plough an area of land agreed upon with King Gylfi of Sweden. It was said that Odin sent Gefjon to visit the king to request ownership of some land. Gylfi, bemused by her request, said that she could claim as much land as she could plough within twenty-four hours. Gefjon thereupon changed her sons into oxen, harnessed them to a plough and turned over a vast area of terrain which she separated from the main land mass. The goddess's oxen sons then dragged the ploughed land out to sea where it became known as Seeland.

Gefjon means the Giving One, and Gebo's meaning is gift.

GEBO'S SYMBOLS
Meaning: Gift
Image: None
Object: Glass
Animal: Ox
Goddess: Gefjon
Tree: None
Colour: Blue

DIVINATORY SIGNIFICANCE
A good partnership or relationship.
Love. Gifts bestowed.

REVERSED*
Emotional problems. Disharmony.

8 Wunjo

The Valkyries

Meaning of symbol: Joy

A drinking vessel, traditionally made out of an animal horn, is seen in the lower area of the picture. This full drinkhorn, which is the symbolic object of Wunjo, is edged and trimmed with gold, and runic glyphs decorate the supporting structure. The signs of Fehu, Uruz, Ansuz, Raido, Gebo and Wunjo are visible.

The sky, flecked with misty shrouds of white cloud, reveals the form of a Valkyry who supports the drinkhorn. The Valkyry's nude figure is caught in a soft golden light which glistens on the horn. Crowned by a mass of red hair which fades to blue in the clouds, her smiling face, with eyes demurely downcast, is framed by two plaits which fall between her breasts. The breasts symbolize that which nurtures and comforts, so the image of female breasts expresses comfort in this rune.

The sign for Wunjo is placed in the upper left corner, in its associated colour of indigo.

There is no deity connected with this rune.

The Valkyries

The Valkyries rode on their steeds to the battlefields and selected valiant warriors who had been slain. The spirits of these heroes were then taken to lead a joyous afterlife in the halls of Valhalla. Their host was Odin and the slain heroes would join him to be given mead that came from the udders of the goat Heidrun. The mead was poured into drinkhorns and served by the thirteen lovely Valkyries. The drinkhorn was thus an expression of the good life enjoyed by the slain heroes.

When refreshed between feasting and drinking, the warriors would spend their time fighting in mock battles, training for their final great conflict of Ragnarök.

The bliss, joy, pleasure and comfort experienced in Valhalla are elements that are emphasized by the rune Wunjo.

WUNJO'S SYMBOLS
Meaning: Joy
Image: Comfort
Object: Drinkhorn
Animal: None
God/Goddess: None
Tree: None
Colour: Indigo

DIVINATORY SIGNIFICANCE
A blessing. Bliss. Devotion. Yearning.
Be wary of pleasure in excess.

REVERSED
For the next few days be wary in business matters.
Impatience. Uncertainty. Strong impulse.

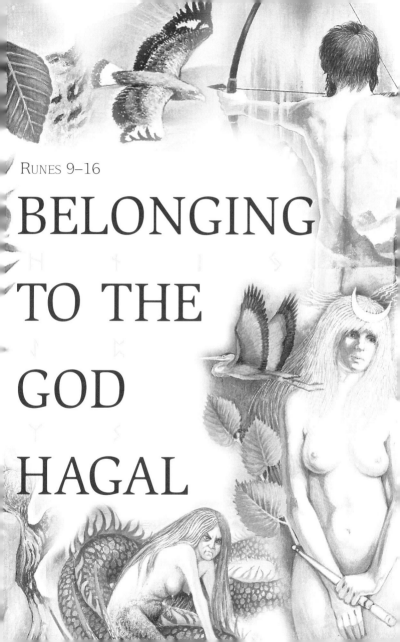

BELONGING

TO THE

GOD

HAGAL

ᚺ

9 Hagalaz

The goddess Hella
Meaning of symbol: Hail

The hideous figure of Hella looms out of the chill mists of Niflheim, her realm of the dead. Her expression is foreboding and her pale shoulders hunch forward revealing the light of her breasts and back, which contrasts with the dark decay of her lower torso.

The dragon Nidhögg, with his gnashing jaws, symbolizes destruction, which is an expression of this rune. Hella is on Nidhögg's back, and the dragon's body, writhing in the swirling mist, forms part of the ground. Human remains are visible in the uncertain light and hail lashes down from the gloomy sky. Just visible in the darkness beyond are the towering walls of Éljúdnir, the hall of Hella, the home of the dead. Tortuous steps lead up to the gates of this grim abode.

In the upper right-hand corner of this image the sign of Hagalaz can be seen. This rune is shown in its associated colour of indigo.

The Goddess Hella

Hella is the goddess associated with Hagalaz. She is the goddess of death and the underworld. Her father Loki and the giantess Angrboda produced two other monsters – Fenris Wolf and the snake Jörmungand.

Hella is a monster woman with an upper body that is pale pink but with a lower body that is a dark, decaying greenish black.

Hella's realm of Hel is surrounded by a swirling death mist and is littered with corpses. This goddess's task is to look after all those who died of illness or old age rather than tending to those who died as heroes on the battlefield.

This rune signifies situations beyond control, both physical and psychological, so what better goddess than Hella to express such events, for her realm is a destination for those who have died of sickness and old age, expressions of the uncontrollable forces of decay and death.

On a psychological or spiritual level, this rune can express the death of the old self as an awakening to a deeper reality manifests.

HAGALAZ'S SYMBOLS
Meaning: Hail
Image: Destruction
Object: None
Animal: None
Goddess: Hella
Tree: None
Colour: Indigo

DIVINATORY SIGNIFICANCE
Uncontrolled forces, either psychological or physical. A message concerning some disruption that is beyond control. Natural events could affect plans for the months or year ahead. Upsets. Risks.

REVERSED*
Negativity. Beyond control.

10 Nauthiz

Tree spirits
Meaning of symbol: Need

A mighty beech tree spreads its noble branches in a clearing, its roots spreading across the ground. Within the trunk of this tree can be seen the subtle female form of the tree spirit.

To the lower left is a sprig of beech with two female flowers. On the left, in the space between two branches, is the sign of the Nauthiz rune, shown in its associated colour of indigo.

This mature beech tree has special significance for the artist who, when living under extremely restricted circumstances with her husband in Kent, was guided to this tree to receive spiritual comfort. This particular tree therefore is associated with restriction, one of the themes symbolized by Nauthiz.

The meaning of this rune is need, which can be seen in the context of a need for material restraint. But this rune can also indicate a spiritual need.

There is no god or goddess associated with this rune.

Trees and Tree Spirits

There are many cultures that believed (and still do believe) in tree spirits and the importance of one particular tree growing within or near a community.

From ancient times individual trees or woodlands have been identified with the spirit forms residing within them. As the home of a particular deity, certain trees were regarded as sacred. For example, the early Egyptians revered the sycamore from where their goddess Hathor gave succour to the souls of the departed.

Trees have been depicted as the axis of heaven and earth, and in Norse legend there is of course the world tree Yggdrasil whose roots gave shelter at the time of Ragnarök.

Still observed in some areas today is the custom of the village elder visiting a mature tree to give the latest community news to the resident tree spirit, at the same time asking the spirit to bless and guide the villagers.

Now, here is something that you can try if you are feeling 'under the weather', either physically or mentally. Go and sit with your back against your favourite tree and absorb the tree's healing energy. You should take with you a token amount of water for the tree's roots. The water, as well as being an expression of thanks, is also for the well-being of the tree.

NAUTHIZ'S SYMBOLS
Meaning: Need
Image: Constraint
Object: None
Animal: None
God/Goddess: None
Tree: Beech
Colour: Indigo

DIVINATORY SIGNIFICANCE
Restrictions. Measured response. Plan carefully.
The necessity to use restraint.

REVERSED*
Unfortunate decision. Unsuitable behaviour or
situation. Covetous or greedy attitude.

NOTE
An increasing number of people are dedicating new trees to loved
ones who have passed on. A tree is a living memorial and a unique
and special way to remember someone dear. The planting of such trees
also helps considerably to create woodland in selected areas. To find
out more about this project in the UK you can contact the Woodland
Trust; Plantit 2000 runs a tree-planting scheme in the USA (see Useful
Addresses at the back of this book).

I

11 Isa

The goddess Skadi
Meaning of symbol: Ice

The snowy, ice-bound Norwegian landscape features the Trollheimen range of mountains which rise chill beneath the dark winter sky.

The giant goddess Skadi rests, curled and sleeping, her body shaping part of the snow-covered slopes as her form rises into the sky. Skadi's hair flows on either side of her face like windswept clouds. The restful features, with eyes closed, merge into shadow. Her arms fold protectively toward her breasts. Her hips turn to her left, the lower line of her thigh forms the contour of the lower slopes before which the diminutive figure of a traveller moves on skis as he pulls a sled.

In the foreground is a reindeer, the totem animal of Isa. This familiar winter symbol in a number of old-world cultures is seen here with its head down to show the spread of antlers.

To the lower left a sprig of alder expresses the tree identified with this rune. To the right is the Isa symbol, shown in its associated colour of black.

The Goddess Skadi

Skadi, the winter goddess, was the very beautiful daughter of Thjazi. She married the god Njörd who liked to live by the seashore at Nóatún and hear the waves crashing and the gulls crying. Skadi, though, preferred the wolves, wind, snow and icy mountain peaks of Thrymheim. Eventually, Njord consented to live with her at Thrymheim for nine nights out of every twelve. She would live with him at Nóatún for the remaining three nights, so these two became the Scandinavian symbols of winter and summer, nine months for winter and three for summer.

The divinatory emphasis of this rune is of progress being blocked, and an expression of such a situation is symbolized by the behaviour of Skadi who held an overwhelming grievance against Thor for killing her father Thjazi. Such was Skadi's obsessive hatred that it prevented her from thinking about anything in a balanced manner. The gods' solution to relieving her blocked mental state was to allow her to choose a husband and then find a way to make Skadi laugh. This was a difficult task considering the mood of the 'ice maiden' goddess, but Loki the prankster succeeded and the problem was solved.

ISA'S SYMBOLS
Meaning: Ice
Image: Reinforce
Object: Ski, sled
Animal: Reindeer
Goddess: Skadi
Tree: Alder
Colour: Black

DIVINATORY SIGNIFICANCE
Taking a step backward. Withdrawn. Progress halted.
A chill response. A parting. A lack of drive.

REVERSED*
Infidelity. Treachery.

In a card layout, Isa reinforces adjacent runes.

12 Jera

The goddess Sif

Meaning of symbol: Year

The spirit form of the beautiful corn goddess Sif is observed in a state of repose. Her long fair hair falls in profusion over her shoulders and around her breasts. Her hair, which becomes one with the ripe corn, is symbolic of a golden harvest. A wreath of corn, supported by her left hand, is worn like a crown on her head, which is inclined to her left. Sif's eyes are closed in sleep, expressing the time of darkness when the crop seeds are germinating. Sif's right arm rests across her abdomen, protecting the source of new life, and her hand sways the waving crop over her thigh. At the same time this hand also supports the image of a traditional scythe with which man will harvest her crop. The scythe, an object associated with this rune, is a symbol of the passage of time, and a twelve-month period is the meaning and one of the divinatory expressions of this rune. The sign of Jera is placed within the cleft of the scythe.

The colour of this rune is black, representing the seed that grows in the darkness; the night before the dawning of life.

The Goddess Sif

Sif, the wife of Thor and the goddess associated with Jera, was the personification of the earth. With her long golden hair that expressed an abundant harvest, this earth mother was identified with the growing and ripening of the crops from spring through summer. Sif, together with her son Uller the winter god, completed the growing cycle.

The symbolic rape of Sif, when Loki cut off her hair, was a dire threat to the continuity of the life-supporting crops. The day was saved though when Loki was forced to redress the situation and told the dwarf Dvalin to make new hair from the finest magical gold thread. Loki's malicious act had so enraged Sif's husband Thor that he had threatened to give Loki a severe beating unless he made amends for his act of violation. This drama, which was settled by discussion, symbolizes legal matters, which have divinatory significance with this rune.

JERA'S SYMBOLS

Meaning: Year

Image: Plenty

Object: Scythe

Animal: None

Goddess: Sif

Tree: None

Colour: Black

DIVINATORY SIGNIFICANCE

A one-year period. Gaining what is rightfully yours.
A professional person. Legal matters.
Obligations. Harmony.

REVERSED*

Taking a situation stage by stage.
Completion cannot be rushed.

13 Eihwaz

The god Uller

Meaning of symbol: Yew

Shown here, at Vestfjorden off Svolvaer in Norway, is a winter landscape of snow-covered mountains and chill waters, from which rises the form of the winter god Uller. He faces away toward the distant mountains, the muscles of his back tense as he aims an arrow with his bow. The bow is the symbolic object associated with Eihwaz. Uller's hair and beard are brown and his skin is warm against the cold mountains.

This god is associated with the mystical lights in the northern skies known as Aurora Borealis. These glorious lights are portrayed here, their colours reflecting in the water, on Uller's bow, and also tinging the snow.

In the foreground by the land at the lower left, a sprig of yew is seen. The yew, which is a symbol of immortality, is associated with Eihwaz. This rune's sign is placed to the upper right of the scene and shown in its associated colour of black.

The God Uller (or Ull)

Uller, who is associated with Eihwaz, was the son of Sif and Orvandil, one of the frost giants. Uller's stepfather was Sif's husband, Thor.

Uller, the winter god, eventually married Skadi the winter goddess. Uller's name meant the Brilliant One and by contrast his mate Skadi was the Shadow.

In early times Uller was considered to be as important as the mighty Odin, and during the winter he ruled over Asgard, the realm of the gods. Each year he was invoked to cover the land in a protective blanket of snow in order to guarantee a good harvest for the coming year.

As the god of hunting and archery, Uller is often shown with a bow and arrows. He loved a successful hunt, and the hunt is one of the symbols of this rune. Uller lived in Ýdalir, the vale of yews. His favoured tree was the yew, which produces the best wood for making bows.

EIHWAZ'S SYMBOLS

Meaning: Yew

Image: The hunt

Object: Bow

Animal: None

God: Uller

Tree: Yew

Colour: Black

DIVINATORY SIGNIFICANCE

A situation resolved. Conflicts can be overcome.
Tenacity.

REVERSED*

A lack of progress. The danger of defeat. Stress.

14 Pertho

The goddess Frigg
Meaning of symbol: Womanhood

The nude spirit figure of the goddess Frigg rises to the right. She wears her traditional crescent moon headdress at her brow. The crescent moon presents a central adornment to Frigg's long fair hair, which falls beyond her shoulders.

The goddess's opalescent white skin reflects moonlight and the slight swelling of her abdomen indicates that she might be pregnant. Across her hips a distaff is held in her left hand. The distaff can be seen as a male fertility symbol, but it is also used to describe the female side of the family – the distaff side. Female concerns and fertility are elements of divinatory significance with this rune.

Near the tip of the distaff there is a sprig of elm, which represents the tree from which the first woman was made. The elm is Pertho's tree.

Flying at Frigg's shoulder level is a heron, by tradition a bird of the morning, and so the cycle of night and day is completed. The heron is associated with Pertho.

In the lower left-hand corner of this scene is the rune sign for Pertho, shown in its symbolic colour of green.

The expression on this goddess's face is gentle and she looks lost in thought. Frigg was depicted in Norse mythology as the introvert to contrast with Odin's extrovert character.

The Goddess Frigg (or Frigga)

Frigg, the queen of the heavens was the wife and consort of Odin, who was the father of her twins – Baldur, the god of spring and the sun, and his opposite, Hödur, a god of darkness. She also bore Hermod, a swift young messenger god.

Frigg was invoked by women giving birth. This was because she was the perfect wife and mother figure.

This goddess is often depicted wearing a crescent moon at her brow and holding a distaff, with a spindle and sometimes with a spinning wheel that is producing long webs of sunset clouds or gold thread. The latter was woven by the three Norns for each person's web of life, but Frigg was responsible for the prima materia.

Frigg is also shown at times with a ring of keys, symbolizing the responsibility of the housewife.

This goddess was aware of what the future would bring but she did not prophesy.

She was renowned for her knowledge and for her discretion as a trustworthy confidante. Pertho, which is Frigg's rune, expresses the collective unconscious that uncovers hidden knowledge.

The goddesses Frigg and Freya, as Janet and Stewart Farrar tell the reader in *The Witches' Goddess*, seem at some time to have been one and the same. This goddess then became two separate entities.

The constellation known as Orion's Girdle is sometimes called Frigg's Spinning Wheel.

PERTHO'S SYMBOLS

Meaning: Womanhood

Image: Fertility

Object: Distaff

Animal: Woman and heron

Goddess: Frigg

Tree: Elm

Colour: Green

DIVINATORY SIGNIFICANCE

Fertility. Female concerns. Creativity.
A surprise. Acquisition. A secret.
A conundrum. Seductive. Discretion.

REVERSED

High expectations can lead to dissatisfaction.
Secrets betrayed.

15 Algiz

The god Heimdal

Meaning of symbol: Defence

The upper torso of the god Heimdal fills the winter landscape.

Heimdal listens intently with an alert and watchful expression. His blowhorn is held poised near his lips in readiness to sound a warning. A warning has divinatory significance with this rune.

Heimdal's crescent-shaped horn is depicted against a night-time sky, but behind his head the sky turns to day. This emphasis of day and night expresses Heimdal's constant duty as the watchman and guardian of the gods.

Heimdal's left arm curves protectively round an elk, the animal associated with this rune. This creature, who possesses a fine spread of defensive antlers, is seen in the foreground. Protection is an element associated with Algiz.

In the lower left corner, a sprig of lime with leaves and berries is shown. The lime belongs to this rune.

Above, at the right-hand corner, set against the daytime sky, the symbol of Algiz is represented in its colour correspondence of green.

The God Heimdal

Heimdal was the son of nine maidens and Odin. The god Odin wed all nine maidens, who simultaneously gave birth to Heimdal. The child swiftly grew to maturity and the wise and handsome Heimdal was chosen by the gods to guard the rainbow bridge Bifrost and to take note of all who passed.

The gods gave Heimdal the gifts of acute hearing and clear sight so that he could be alert both during the day and at night. Because he required little sleep, he became the watchman of the gods.

Heimdal possessed a gleaming sword and a golden-maned horse, but his most important possession was the blowhorn that he used to sound a warning when the enemies of the gods approached. He also blew a soft note upon the instrument to announce the presence of the gods on the rainbow bridge. Though soft, this note was loud enough to be heard throughout the nine worlds.

The horn was kept safe and secure in the branches of the world tree Yggdrasil or beneath the water of Mimir's Well. When the horn was in the well it became the symbol of the new moon, whilst the eye that Odin sacrificed became the symbol of the full moon as the horn and the eye lay side by side.

At the time of the final world conflict, Heimdal slew the god Loki. These two gods, who were exact opposites, destroyed each other during the conflagration.

When Christianity gained influence and power, Heimdal became St Michael.

ALGIZ'S SYMBOLS

Meaning: Defence

Image: To protect

Object: Blowhorn

Animal: Elk

God: Heimdal

Tree: Lime

Colour: Green

DIVINATORY SIGNIFICANCE

A new position gained by effort or reward. A new job or pursuit will stimulate your intellect. A warning. Protection.

REVERSED

Mislead. Beware of those who would take advantage of you. A weak position. Proceed with caution.

ϟ

16 Sowulo

The god Baldur
Meaning of symbol: Sun

A sunset bathes the landscape and rippling waters in a golden orange glow. The sun can be seen in the cleft of mountains on the horizon. These silhouetted crags are in the area of Reine in Lofoten, Norway.

The solar god Baldur is seen in the foreground. His fair hair and blue eyes reflect the sunlight too. He has a tender expression as he gazes across the top of his circular shield, the object associated with this rune.

The shield, with a domed metal boss at its centre, has four quarter sections which are divided by stitched skin coverings. Baldur's shield can be seen as a sun symbol, and also as a symbol of eternity and the four seasons. The seasons are represented by the quarter sections.

The runic symbol for Sowulo, in its colour correspondence of green, is shown across one of the shield's sections.

An eagle, the animal associated with this rune, flies above the water shedding rays of light from its wings. According to ancient folk lore, the eagle, a solar symbol for several ancient civilizations and the king of the birds, is reputedly immune from death.

The oak is Sowulo's tree, and a sprig of oak with an acorn can be seen in the lower right-hand corner.

The God Baldur (or Balder)

Baldur the sun god is associated with Sowulo which is also a symbol of the life-giving sun.

Baldur was the gentle and much-loved son of Odin and Frigg. He was also loved by gods and men alike for his wisdom, gentleness, mercy and his ability to make sound judgements. By contrast, creating the negative to Baldur's positive, the solar god's twin brother Hödur was sombre, sullen and blind.

There were some who believed that the summer and winter seasons were created by the power of the two brothers and that, as the days grew shorter after the summer solstice, Baldur gradually faded under the growing influence of Hödur, who reigned in the dark winter months. Baldur (like Iduna) would live in the chill depths of the underworld during winter.

Baldur suffered a series of disturbing dreams which made him fear for his life. His fear was realized when he was killed by a lance made by Loki but thrown by his brother Hödur. The lance was fashioned from mistletoe, taken from a plant that grew on an oak tree at the gateway to Valhalla.

There was great grief expressed at Baldur's funeral. and his wife Nanna fell dead so that she could join her husband.

Baldur's death heralded the coming of Ragnarök, but the sun god rose again in the new world.

The summer solstice festival used to remember Baldur's death and the fading of the light. With the coming of Christianity, this sun god was replaced by St John.

SOWULO'S SYMBOLS

Meaning: Sun
Image: Life-force
Object: Shield
Animal: Eagle
God: Baldur
Tree: Oak
Colour: Green

DIVINATORY SIGNIFICANCE

Relax and rest. Take care of your health. Clarity. Clear vision. Achievement.

REVERSED*

Egotistical. Self-centred.

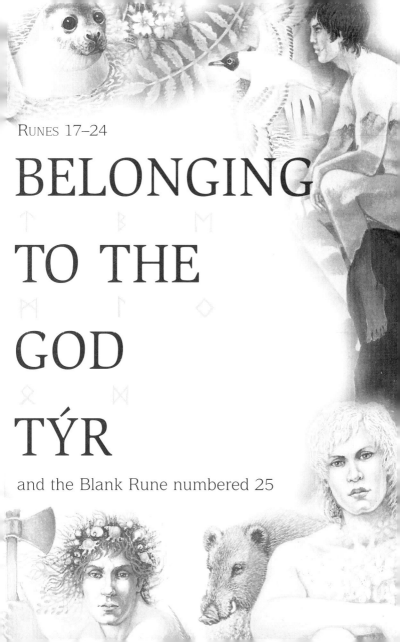

BELONGING TO THE GOD TÝR

and the Blank Rune numbered 25

↑

17 Teiwaz

The god Týr
Meaning of symbol: Victory

The figure of the god Týr looms like a dark cloud over a mountainous landscape. Týr's windswept head is bowed forward, his eyes are closed and his bearded face is half hidden by the hilt of a massive shining sword. In his left hand he holds the handle with the blade pointing down. His right hand crosses toward the hilt but the hand is lost from view, indicating the sacrifice that he has made. The sword symbolizes supreme power, vitality, strength, justice and divine truth. This links in with the meaning and image of Teiwaz: to triumph in legal matters. Below Týr are the Lakselvtindan Peaks in Lyngen, Norway. The tip of Týr's golden sword hangs over the still water in the foreground, where there is a sprig of hazel with two nuts. The hazel tree is associated with this rune.

At the top right is the symbol of Teiwaz, seen in its associated colour of yellow, which reflects warm light on the snow-covered mountains.

The God Týr (or Tiu)

Týr, the god of defence and justice and the patron god of the sword, has roots going back to early Indo-European history. He was, to the majority of the Germanic people, the original sky god. Sometimes he was portrayed as Zio, in a twin, dual-gender role, to express both a male and female aspect. According to Icelandic mythology he had no consort, but nevertheless some reference is made to his wife being Angurboda the giantess.

Týr was the only god to approach and feed the awesome Fenris Wolf. He sacrificed his right hand when bitten by Fenris Wolf, but was able to fight just as well with one hand. Knowing one's true strength and using this knowledge to good effect, which is one of the meanings indicated by Teiwaz, is seen in Týr's action when the evil Fenris Wolf had to be contained. He had the strength of character to do what had to be done.

Týr was the epitome of all that was honourable. His leadership qualities and concern for humanity were recognized when he was honoured by being made one of the council of twelve gods.

Týr was invoked for arbitration, law and order, the swearing of oaths, battle and bravery.

TEIWAZ'S SYMBOLS

Meaning: Victory
Image: A legal win
Object: Sword
Animal: None
God: Týr
Tree: Hazel
Colour: Yellow

DIVINATORY SIGNIFICANCE

You know where your true strengths lie so make
use of this knowledge. General success is indicated.
A possible legal advantage. Honour. Leadership.
A love-smitten man, if the enquirer is male.
If the enquirer is female, great love will be hers.

REVERSED

An untrustworthy relationship.
Complications in romance.

18 Berkana

The goddess Urd
Meaning of symbol: Growth

The cloaked figure of the elderly Urd, one of the three Norns, stands to the right. She looks back over her shoulder, with long tresses of white wispy hair catching in the wind, as she holds her cloak protectively about her. Behind Urd the sky is cloudy with a hint of pink beyond the blue-grey cloud forms.

To Urd's rear a polar bear moves forward to gaze at the onlooker. The bear, totem animal for Berkana, is a familiar symbol of strength in ancient beliefs; for example, the Greek goddess of the hunt Athena has been portrayed in the company of bears, and Odin often appeared as one. The polar bear here links with the animals seen in the most northern areas of Norway.

The snowy form of a swan, symbol of gentleness, purity and grace, rises from below, its neck gracefully curved and its wings partly unfurled. The white swan is also an expression of the silence of the three Norns at the time of Ragnarök. The three sisters were able to appear as swans and they also tended the two swans upon the waters of the Urdar Fountain.

A sprig of birch with a leaf and catkin can be seen in the lower left corner. The birch is Berkana's tree.

The rune symbol for Berkana is shown at the top left corner in its colour correspondence of yellow.

The Goddess Urd

Urd is the goddess associated with the rune Berkana. She is also one of the three Norns. Urd and her sisters Verdandi and Skuld respectively represented the past, present and future.

These three sisters cared for two swans that swam upon the Urdar Fountain, and legend relates that all swans are descended from this pair. When the Norns visited the earth, they were said to wear the plumage of swans. To contact mortals, they appeared as mermaids in order to impart their wisdom.

Orlog, the everlasting law of the universe, directed the Norns to weave webs of fate. The sisters worked on webs so huge that they stretched from the mountains of the east to the far reaches of the western seas. As the three goddesses worked they solemnly chanted.

Urd, the eldest of the three, imparted knowledge and wisdom gained from past events. She constantly looked back over her shoulder. If the three sisters were together, Urd would be facing in the opposite direction to Skuld, her sister of the future.

The three Norns are also known as the wyrd or weird sisters and they are the source of many stories that involve groupings of three witches, such as Shakespeare's *Macbeth*.

The birch, which is a symbol for this rune, is one of several trees, including the ash and willow, that have significance in witchcraft to this day.

Berkana is a rune signifying growth. Growth can be seen on the level of a family growing and expanding, on a material level, or on a spiritual level as growth of the self.

BERKANA'S SYMBOLS

Meaning: Growth

Image: Enterprise

Object: None

Animal: Bear and swan

Goddess: Urd

Tree: Birch

Colour: Yellow

DIVINATORY SIGNIFICANCE

The family. A member of the family. Motherhood.
News of a birth. Rebirth. Fertility.

REVERSED

An upset with a member of the family.
Family problems. Anxiety.

ᛗ

19 Ehwaz

The goddess Iduna
Meaning of symbol: Horse

The spirit figure of the young goddess Iduna lies back with knees raised. She is bathed in a warm light and her fair hair casts a shadow over her eyes. Her right arm follows the sensual curve of her body and a golden apple is supported in her fingers.

In the lower left foreground a box shape reflects all the colours of the rainbow. This receptacle, appearing transparent against Iduna's arm, represents the box in which the goddess kept her apples of eternal youth.

The horse, strongly linked to this rune, leaps up and forward above the goddess. The creature's legs and hooves appear as ghostly shadows by Iduna's curved knees and the animal's mane flows toward the sign of Ehwaz. According to ancient lore, the horse, due to its speed and energy, became associated with the journey of the sun, the supreme life-force. This association creates a link with Iduna, Ehwaz's deity.

The colour of this rune is in shades of yellow, set against a dramatic sky.

The Goddess Iduna

The young and lovely Iduna was the goddess of eternal youth. Some believed that this goddess had no birth but just a continuing existence.

Iduna married Bragi, who was elected by Odin to be the creator of the music and song that would celebrate the heroes and gods of Valhalla.

Iduna enjoyed the duty of picking and distributing the golden apples of eternal youth. Only she was allowed to pick these apples, which grew on the Tree of Life, Knowledge and Experience, guarded by the three Norns. Iduna carried her magical golden apples in a wooden box made of ash. She promised the gods that she would give them daily supplies of these apples, which had the power to impart immortal health and beauty. Her wooden box was always full, no matter how many apples she distributed.

Iduna belongs to one of the older group of deities.

EHWAZ'S SYMBOLS
Meaning: Horse
Image: Confirmation
of life-force
Object: Box
Animal: Horse
Goddess: Iduna
Tree: Apple
Colour: Yellow

DIVINATORY SIGNIFICANCE
A home change brings improvement.
Progress. Reliability.

REVERSED
Travel across water. Traumatic changes.
Timing. When to act.

In a card layout, Ehwaz reinforces adjacent runes.

20 Mannaz

The All-Father
Meaning of symbol: Man

The head and bare chest of a dark-haired man are seen in the lower section of this vision. His bearded face, which has a peaceful expression, is turned slightly to one side and his eyes are closed in reflective thought. The man is representative of the species (homo sapiens) that has gained supremacy over other creatures because of its power of reason.

On the left, above and behind this man appears the blue-cloaked figure of the All-Father Odin. The blue-grey eyes of the god gaze forward as if focused on a distant horizon. His silver hair is seen from beneath the hood of his cloak and his moustache frames a determined set of the mouth and jawline.

Odin is shown here before he sacrificed one of his eyes to the Well of Mimir in order to gain wisdom, thus reflecting the decisions and sacrifices to be made by a man during his lifetime.

The self and a state of reflection are elements that have strong divinatory significance with this rune.

Odin appears in this Rune Vision Card only as a symbol of the intuitive god-like spirit within mortal man, for there is no god or goddess image attached to this rune.

The hawk's head, seen crowning this card, represents the symbolic bird of the rune Mannaz. The hawk is seen as a creature that can think clearly before taking action, so this bird can be seen as another expresion of reflective thought. It also expressed the physical link between earth and the realm of the gods. Odin was able to transform himself into this predatory creature.

In the lower right-hand corner the rune sign for Mannaz is shown in its corresponding colour of orange.

MANNAZ'S SYMBOLS

Meaning: Man/Woman/
Human being

Image: Species

Object: Man

Animal: Hawk

God/Goddess: None

Tree: None

Colour: Orange

DIVINATORY SIGNIFICANCE

Self. Reflection. Modesty. Humanitarian attitude.
Delay signing any legal paper or contract
if you are undecided.

REVERSED

Be warned of an enemy. The next rune will guide
you on how to act. Selfish. Egotistical.

NOTE

The artist would like to dedicate this image to her husband Leon Olin,
as a thank-you for the years thay have shared.

ᛚ

21 Laguz

The god Njörd

Meaning of symbol: Water

Njörd, the god of the seas and the god associated with the rune Laguz, rises from the rippling water, his torso caught in a golden morning light. He gazes steadfastly toward an unseen horizon. His hair, ruffled by a sea breeze, is adorned with seashells and seaweed. He is shown, traditionally, in the prime of life. To indicate water as the life source, Njörd's right hand is directed down to the sea's surface. His fingers fade, changing in appearance to that of a waterfall. In his left hand he holds an axe, an implement that symbolizes both battle and work. A sprig of willow is by the god's left shoulder. The willow tree is associated with the location of water and it is the tree that is connected with Laguz.

In the ocean below, a mother seal and her pup gaze inquisitively. They are unafraid as Njörd protects them. Above flies a seagull. Both creatures are beloved by Njörd. Intuition and psychic ability are divinatory meanings attached to this rune These gifts are expressed through Njörd's communication with the birds and the creatures of the ocean. At the top right of this scene is the runic symbol of Laguz in its associated colour of orange. This colour is associated with fire, an element that Njörd controlled along with the wind and the waves.

The God Njörd (or Niörd)

Njörd, the husband of Skadi, the father of Frey and Freya, and the god associated with this rune, was the deity of the seas that bordered the shoreline and the god of the winds whose force he controlled. Njörd was also the patron god of seafarers. He blessed them and also protected their ships and cargoes, enabling them to pass to and from safe harbours. This god is often depicted with a crown of shells and seaweed. All ocean plant life near the shores belonged to him. Njörd was also linked to the harvest of the land as well as that of the sea. His palace of Nóatún stood near the shoreline and he came to dwell, at first as a hostage, in Asgard, after a battle had raged between the gods.

Njörd attended all the great meetings of the gods and he was selected to be one of the twelve that took their place in the great council hall of Asgard.

LAGUZ'S SYMBOLS

Meaning: Water

Image: Source

Object: Axe

Animal: Seal and seagull

God: Njörd

Tree: Willow

Colour: Orange

DIVINATORY SIGNIFICANCE

Intuition. Psychic ability. Use your psychic insight.
Acquisition. A successful pursuit. Birth.

REVERSED

Work within your limitations.

22 Inguz

The god Frey
Meaning of symbol: Virility

The face of the young god Frey expresses a mixture of tenderness and strength. He has blue eyes and fair hair, the same colouring as his beautiful sister Freya. He sits amidst a golden crop of barley and clover, supporting himself on his left arm, in front of which rises up a yellow iris. His right arm rests forward on his right knee. The fingers of his hand are tinged with green. His torso is decorated with apple blossoms, sea rocket and forget-me-nots. Primroses spring from his left thigh. In the language of flowers primroses symbolize life anew. Following the form of his right leg is a plant of the arum family, which is also known as lords and ladies. Frey is known as the Lord and his sister as the Lady. This plant is also known as cuckoo-pint, and below it we see a cuckoo, one of the creatures associated with Inguz. The cuckoo, symbol of the approaching spring, is thus a harbinger of the future and represents the soul of new life. An inverted helmet rests on the ground between Frey's legs, its form suggesting the erect male organ. This was a traditional way of portraying this god. By Frey's right shoulder, his golden-bristled boar, Gullinbursti, thrusts his head over the crop.

In the soft blue skies can be seen the rune sign of Inguz, shown in its colour correspondence of orange.

The God Frey

Frey, the son of Njörd, was a fertility god. He was also a god of sunlight, peace and prosperity, and the patron of horses and riders.

Because of a treaty with the gods, Frey and his sister Freya came to live in Asgard to be with their father Njörd.

Whilst still a baby, and to celebrate his first tooth, Frey was given the realm of Álfheim where he was to live and rule with love over the light elves and faeries. Here we see the expression of the family, expectations for a growing family and caring concern, all of which have divinatory significance when this rune is drawn.

As an expression of male fertility, statues of Frey often portray this god with an erect penis. His magical sword is also a symbol of male fertility.

Frey has yet another connection with Inguz, which is the completion of a project, symbolized in his battle with the giant Surt.

Frey is also attributed with bringing forth light from darkness; this can be seen on different levels, including the curing and easing of mental depression, a factor which has divinatory significance with this rune.

Frey and his sister Freya are amongst those gods and goddesses who are surrounded by a multitude of legends.

INGUZ'S SYMBOLS
Meaning: Virility
Image: Male fertility
Object: Helmet
Animal: Boar and cuckoo
God: Frey
Tree: None
Colour: Orange

DIVINATORY SIGNIFICANCE
Male fertility. Expectations for family,
children and health. The completion of a project.
A mental state is resolved.

REVERSED*
Conclusions and beginnings. Stages of progress.

23 Othila

The god Váli

Meaning of symbol: To inherit

This scene is viewed from the heights of the rocks of Troll Mountain at Svolvaer in Lofoten, Norway. This remarkable natural stone forms a mighty seat, like a rugged throne, upon which sits the youthful god Váli, who, although young, expresses confidence and maturity. He leans forward with his face in profile, gazing across the distant landscape. The power of his spirit form shimmers blue through the rock upon which he sits, so that he becomes as one with the stone. The classical symbolism of rocks is invariably an expression of that which is eternal and steadfast. Rocks of a curious and unique formation are also legendary places for sheltering and harbouring spirit forms, so this Troll Mountain formation is an ideal throne for Váli who is destined to reign in the next world after Ragnarök. The seat is the object associated with this rune. Below Váli are the lands and waters of the world whose ending he is destined to survive.

The rune Othila, which is placed to the lower right of the scene, is shown in its traditional red. The theme of inheritance –

which can be seen in the context of a birthright inheritance or obligation – is expressed in the landscape and the elevated position of the Troll Mountain rock. Othila's image is 'estate', which links with inheritance and land.

The God Váli

Váli was the son of Odin and Rind. A remarkable aspect of Váli the infant was that he developed with such amazing speed that he reached his full mature height within the first day of his life. This god of everlasting light, who was a symbol of vegetation growing after the chilled winter soil has been warmed by the sun, was also known as Váli the Avenger because Váli made it his purpose to avenge Baldur's death. He set out to hunt down and kill Hödur the sightless god of darkness who had been tricked into killing Baldur. The vengeance killing of Hodur symbolized the clearing away of the winter darkness to bring light. Váli took his seat in the hall of Gladsheim. He shared his father's home of Valaskiálf, and was one of the gods to survive the end of the world, known as Ragnarök.

Váli is most often represented as an archer so, when change came, the Christian hierarchy replaced him with St Valentine, who was also renowned for his archery and was, like Váli, a messenger of light.

OTHILA'S SYMBOLS
Meaning: To inherit
Image: Estate
Object: Seat
Animal: None
God: Váli
Tree: None
Colour: Red

DIVINATORY SIGNIFICANCE
Inheritance. Legacies. Spiritual heritage.
Land. Property. Wills. Habitation. Fundamental values.

REVERSED
Mechanical equipment may fail.
Damage or an accident.

24 Dagaz

The goddess Verdandi

Meaning of symbol: Day

The cloaked figure of the goddess Verdandi, one of the three Norns, stands in the foreground with the hood of her cloak resting on the back of her mass of red hair.

This all-knowing goddess's features are set in a stern expression as she regards the onlooker with her slanted and hypnotic eyes.

Verdandi raises the Web of Fate protectively towards her; its rainbow colours reflect the daylight and each colour reflects the fates of mankind. Each one of us is caught in its strands.

In the background can be seen the water and mountains of Austnesfjord in Lofoten. Beyond this mountain terrain there are rays of sunlight across the sky. These rays express day which is the meaning of Dagaz. This can be seen as a new dawning, as light coming into your life as you begin a fresh and positive phase. This new chapter may be material, intellectual or spiritual self-transformation.

Another expression of this rune is security, an element that can be seen in the symbolism of the protective mountains which, because they reach up to the heavens, also enjoy a traditional association with the gods.

The tree linked with this rune is rowan, which grows in the Lofoten region. A sprig of rowan with flame-red berries is placed to the side of Verdandi.

The symbol for Dagaz is shown in its colour correspondence of red. It is situated in the upper left corner.

The Goddess Verdandi

Verdandi, the goddess associated with Dagaz, was also one of the three Norns, the sisters of the past, present and future. Verdandi represented the present.

This goddess, with her two sisters Urd and Skuld, lived by the fountain of Urdar. It was here that the gods came to receive answers to their questions. The Norns however remained silent about the fate of these gods and they also kept their peace amidst the devastation of the final conflict known as Ragnarök.

Ragnarök can be seen to symbolize the destruction of the old self as a dramatic self-transformation takes place.

Verdandi and her sister Urd spent much of their time weaving the Web of Fate whilst Skuld sought to destroy their work, so these three reflected the creative and destructive side of nature.

Dagaz, if followed by the blank rune, can sometimes mean death or the end of a phase to make way for a new one;

therefore extreme caution and discretion are needed when interpreting these two runes.

DAGAZ'S SYMBOLS
Meaning: Day
Image: Security
Object: None
Animal: None
Goddess: Verdandi
Tree: Rowan
Colour: Red

DIVINATORY SIGNIFICANCE
Prosperity. Security. Growth. A change of situation for the better. A mental transition.

REVERSED*
A traumatic change. A new perspective.

25 The Blank Rune

The blank rune is the symbol of karma, destiny and fate. This rune can also be interpreted as an omen of death – but not necessarily physical death.

Karma and Reincarnation

Karma is the law of cause and effect; it is also the mainstay of the belief in reincarnation, a philosophy that teaches that we travel through a series of lives in order to reach a state of perfection, at which point we no longer need to reincarnate.

Our stages of progress, or incarnations, are calculated by all our positive and negative actions. Karma therefore reflects every spiritual, material, professional, emotional and sexual aspect of our many lives.

DIVINATORY SIGNIFICANCE

Karma. Cause and effect. Destiny.
Fate. Inevitability. Death. Ending.

REVERSED

None.

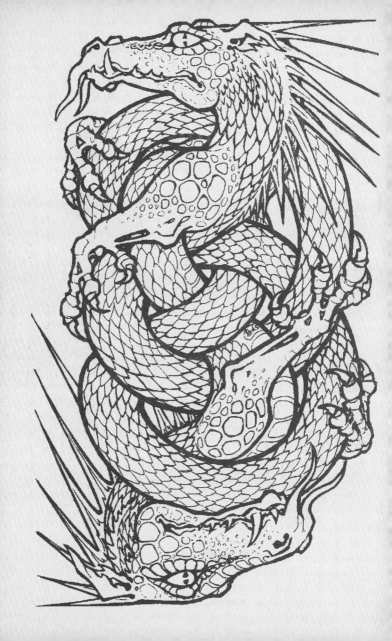

CONSULTING THE ORACLE OF THE RUNES

How to Read the Cards

Setting the Mood for a Reading

Whether you are reading for yourself or for others, it is essential that you create a peaceful and therapeutic atmosphere, especially if you are reading for someone who is having a consultation for the first time and who may be feeling nervous.

What you do not want, prior to and during a reading, is any outside interference or distraction. You should make sure that you are well away from all telephones, television, radio, children and pets. Ideally, your reading room should be an area which is kept solely for consultations.

Other effective aids to relaxation are the burning of subtle incenses or oils and quiet background music that can be faded out when you start a reading.

Last but not least, it is important that you too are in a relaxed state of mind, so always give yourself time to meditate before and after you have given a reading.

Reading the Rune Vision Cards

The same guidelines apply to reading Rune Vision Cards as apply to reading tarot cards.

First of all, become thoroughly familiar with the images and meanings of each Rune Vision Card. This preliminary exercise will also help you to establish a rapport with the cards.

The cards, when spread out in preparation for a reading, should face the reader and not the enquirer. An important point to note with all card layouts is that when turning the cards over and placing them face up, you should establish a routine of turning the cards over sideways and not end over end, which will put the majority of cards into the reversed position! If an unusually high number of cards are in the reversed position, you should start again.

You should never frighten the enquirer with horror predictions. If a serious health condition or death is seen at a reading, these situations must be treated with extreme sensitivity.

The Rune Vision Card interpretations that you should use when giving readings are those that are recorded with each card under the heading of Divinatory Significance. It is these divinatory definitions alone which you should use when consulting the Cards. This point is emphasized to help you avoid confusion with the title meanings and symbolism of each Rune Vision Card. It can be a confusing area at times, as you will see after studying and reading each card's profile, but the golden rule when giving readings is to use only the interpretations listed under Divinatory Significance (and reversed definitions where such apply).

No one can really 'teach' you how to read runes, cards or a crystal. There are only useful technical tips that you can apply with your own psychic ability, which will vary in degree from person to person but which can certainly be developed.

When you have the cards in front of you, use the card interpretations to give you information but allow your intuitive/psychic sensitivity to narrow that information down to specifics. This may be difficult for some at first but amazingly easy for others. When I was being taught to use my psychic abilities, I was taught to trust my first impressions. This may sound like a cliché but it happens to be very good advice, so when you are reading the Rune Vision Cards, get into the habit of being conscious of the first impression that comes to mind as you look at each card.

Confidence is a key factor in successful divining, so use your family, friends and acquaintances as practice subjects.

Cards are very personal, therefore you should never let anyone, other than yourself and the enquirer, touch your cards. Try to keep your Rune Vision Cards in a safe and secure place.

The Three-card Spread

The following spread is an easy and quick layout for someone seeking a solution to a problem.

The enquirer shuffles the cards face down before choosing three, placing them one at a time, face up, from left to right.

The first card represents the enquirer's problem. The second card points to the course of action that should be taken, and the third expresses the outcome.

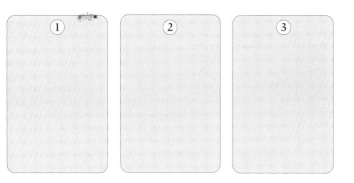

The Celtic Cross Spread

The Celtic Cross spread is not only traditional but it is probably the most popular of tarot card layouts. It is a tried and tested system that is used primarily to answer an enquirer's question. It is also a spread that is perfectly suited to the Rune Vision Cards.

The full deck should be shuffled face down by the reader and then shuffled, still face down, by the enquirer. The enquirer then selects a card from anywhere in the deck and places it face up in the centre of the reading table. This card will represent the enquirer. The reader then selects one card at a time from the top of the deck, following the numbered sequence as illustrated in the Celtic Cross Spread diagram. As each card is placed in position, the reading progresses to a conclusion, as follows:

1. Turn over the first card from the deck and place it on top of the enquirer's card. As you do so, say, 'This covers you.' The first card expresses the atmosphere relating to the enquirer and the enquirer's question.

2. Turn over the second card from the deck and place it across the first. As you do so, say, 'This crosses you.' This card points to forces, either negative or positive, that oppose the enquirer or question.

3. Turn over the third card from the deck and place it above the enquirer. As you do so, say, 'This card expresses the enquirer's ideal wish in connection with the question.'

4. Turn over the fourth card from the deck, placing it below the enquirer. As you do so, say, 'This card indicates the foundation of the subject under discussion.'

5. Turn over the fifth card from the deck, placing it to the left of the enquirer. As you do so, say, 'This is behind you.' This card expresses the enquirer's past.

6. Turn over the sixth card from the deck, placing it to the right of the enquirer. As you do so, say, 'This is before you.' This card expresses the enquirer's future.

7. Turn over the seventh card from the deck, placing it to the right but below the cross that has been formed by the cards that are already in place. As you do so, say, 'This answers you.' This card provides the answer to the question which was the reason for the consultation.

8. Turn over the eighth card from the deck and place it above the seventh. As you do so, say, 'This card expresses individual influences which could help the enquirer.'

9. Turn over the ninth card from the deck and place it above the eighth. As you do so, say, 'This describes you.' This card expresses the personality of the enquirer.

10. Turn over the tenth card from the deck and the last card for this reading. As you do so, say, 'This is the conclusion.' In the event of an inconclusive or ambiguous answer to the question, use the tenth and last card as the enquirer's card for a fresh reading, repeating the sequence as before.

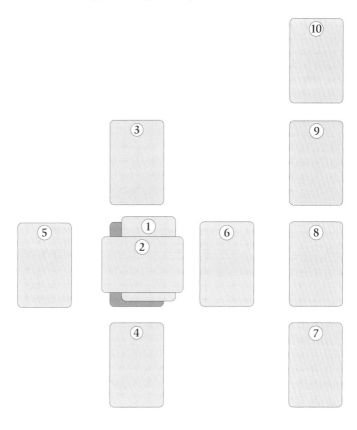

The Twelve-month Runecast

The Twelve-month Runecast, which has been adapted from my Witches Circle Astrology Spread, (see *Tarot of the Old Path* and *Tarot of Northern Shadows*) is a card layout that will provide the enquirer with a one-year forecast.

The reader commences by shuffling the cards face down and then asks the enquirer to choose two cards, still keeping them face down, from anywhere in the deck. The enquirer then starts forming a circle by placing the two chosen cards at the one o'clock position, imagining that the circle represents a clock face. He or she then continues to choose two cards at a time, placing them clockwise until the circle is completed at the twelve o'clock setting. One card is now left and this is placed in the centre of the clock face. This last card represents the enquirer.

The reader begins the consultation by turning over the first two cards at the one o'clock setting. When turning over pairs of cards, the first card to be read in each pair is the card in the inner circle. The next card is therefore the companion card in the outer circle. The one o'clock position is January and, moving clockwise around the circle, you conclude the reading at the twelve o'clock position which is December.

The first two cards that you turn over may well give you the reason or provide the theme for the reading. Kim Tracey always found that the first two runes at January, coupled with the two directly opposite at July, together with the centre rune representing the enquirer, nearly always pointed to the reason for the reading. You could see if this particular pattern has the same significance for you.

You now have examples of three very different card layouts, any one of which should suit you and your enquirers' needs.

At the end of the day the best system of course is the system that is best for you. Practice and experimenting will produce a formula that you find ideal.

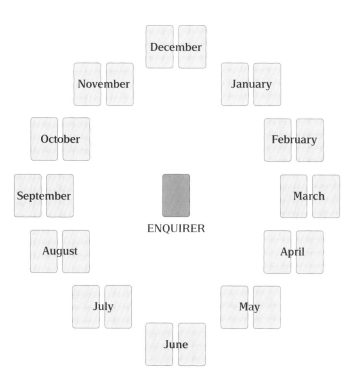

THE SYMBOLS OF THE RUNE VISION CARDS

The Colours and Trees of the Runes

Sylvia Gainsford's Note

Just as the runes express life, so the language of colours and their association with each rune can be explained. Here is a list of the runes and their associated colours:

Red	Purple	Blue	Indigo
Othila	Uruz	Raido	Wunjo
Dagaz	Thurisaz	Kaunaz	Hagalaz
Fehu	Ansuz	Gebo	Nauthiz

Black	Green	Yellow	Orange
Isa	Pertho	Teiwaz	Mannaz
Jera	Algiz	Berkana	Laguz
Eihwaz	Sowulo	Ehwaz	Inguz

The use of colour pigment has long played a part in ancient and modern rituals. Early man applied red pigment spots to corpses and, in recent times, those new to fox hunting have been ritually initiated by being daubed in the face with the blood of the fox.

Red, blue and yellow pigments form the three primary colours that are mixed together by artists to create secondary colours. Together, the primary and secondary colours create a gradated circle of hues that is reflected in the runic cycle, in which the red in the final rune, Dagaz, ultimately flows back to Fehu, the first rune in the sequence. The full range of primary and secondary colours has been described as colouring the cords of the Web of Fate woven by the three Norns. As the colours relate to the workings of the natural world, they and the runes have particular associations with the tree imagery depicted in the cards.

Let us begin by considering the first primary colour: red.

Red

The colour of blood, the flow of life, blood that flows at birth, menstruation, wounding or death in battle.

Red is traditionally the colour of strength and aggression, yet conversely it is associated with love. It is the most vibrant colour of all and the strongest colour to register on the eye.

Red is linked with the runes Fehu (number 1), Othila (number 23) and Dagaz (number 24), so red, at both the beginning and the end, links the cycle of life's activity and completes the cycle of rainbow colours.

The deities linked with these runes, in the same sequence as above, are the goddess Freya, who was much renowned for her prowess in love and battle, the young god Váli, born to avenge the death of Baldur, and finally the Norn Verdandi with her determination and fearless spirit. The language of the colour red is clearly seen in the nature of these beings.

The associated trees for Fehu and Dagaz (there is no tree association for Othila), are elder and rowan. The Scandinavian red-leaved elder gives us an obvious clue with its red berries, and the red-leaved elder's British cousin is a tree much venerated in folklore and witchcraft tradition. Anyone who wants to use the berries, leaves or wood of this tree is strongly advised to ask the tree spirit's permission beforehand ... or suffer the consequences! The bright-red berries of the rowan also give us an obvious clue. By tradition this tree is said to give protection against evil influences

Purple

This secondary colour links red and blue because purple is made by mixing these two primary colours.

Purple is associated with royalty, leadership and therefore power. If red is seen as earthly energy and blue is an expression of heavenly and spiritual matters, then to possess both attributes is truly powerful.

Purple is associated with the runes Uruz (number 2), Thurisaz (number 3) and Ansuz (number 4).

The deities associated with these runes, in the same order as above, are Vidar, Loki and Odin.

Vidar, the 'silent one', was an all-knowing god who was destined to play a part in the final conflict and to survive and rule in the next world.

Loki was a powerful force who opposed Odin. Loki was like the red hearth fire because fire can also be destructive if not kept under control. By contrast, Odin, the leader and ruler of the gods, was associated with the blue of the heavens and spiritual perfection.

The destinies of Odin and Loki were inextricably linked. They represented the negative and positive aspects that must be kept in balance like the destructive and creative elements of nature. And so it is that the red of Loki and the blue of Odin create purple.

The two trees associated with Thurisaz and Ansuz (there is no tree association with Uruz) are blackthorn and ash.

The dark-purple berries of the blackthorn reflect the colour association for these runes, and the branch formation of this tree provides an impenetrable barrier which expresses the reclusive and protective character of Vidar. The fruit and leaves of the blackthorn disguise the presence of long vicious thorns, a reflection of the cruel and mischief-making nature of Loki. In contrast, the blackthorn is one of the first trees to flower. The flowers are pure white and express the earth's physical and spiritual awakening, which can be seen to be linked with the guidance and protection of Odin.

The ash is a truly significant tree for it was from the great world ash tree Yggdrasil that Odin hung, impaled on his own spear, in order to gain the wisdom of the dead and the knowledge of the runes.

In ancient Norse belief, the world had nine regions placed within a tricentric structure comparable to heaven, earth and hell. Heaven was known as Asgard. Earth, the middle level, was called Midgard. These two levels were linked by the flaming rainbow bridge Bifrost.

The last and lower region was referred to as Niflheim, a misty world of the dead. In this land of the dead there was another realm called Hel which was administered by an abominable female named Hella.

Sheltering this world with its different levels was the mighty ash tree Yggdrasil. Three huge roots grew out from the ash. One root stretched down to Niflheim, another root curled into Midgard and the remaining root was in Asgard.

The first male and female humans were made from ash and elm. They were named Ask and Embla.

The male flowers of the ash tree are dark purple and they appear before the leaves.

Blue

This colour is associated with spiritual energy because it is the colour of the sky where the gods dwelt in Asgard. The sky is reflected by blue waters, so blue is linked with light and life. Blue also expresses the eternity of the universe, and it is the colour of purity, spirituality and spiritual protection.

Blue is linked with the runes Raido (number 5), Kaunaz (number 6) and Gebo (number 7).

The deities linked with these runes, in the same sequence as above, are Thor, Skuld and Gefjon.

Thor rode across the sky in his airborne chariot with blue lightning streaks flashing from his hammer, so the association of blue with this god is quite obvious. Blue also expresses his strength of spirit.

The Norn Skuld swept across the sky with the Valkyries, so here we have another connection with the blue of the sky.

Gefjon, 'the giving one', was the goddess of pure virgins and so she represented the spiritual purity of blue.

The tree associations with Raido and Kaunaz (there is no tree association with Gebo) are oak and pine.

Oak is an important tree in symbolism and venerated by the Druids. This tree, because of its own natural characteristics, reflects endurance, strength and immortality. It is a common myth that lightning is attracted to the oak, and so grew the association between this particular tree and the gods of lightning, in this case Thor. The oak is sacred to this popular deity.

Pine is also a much revered tree. The blue-green needle-like leaves are retained throughout the year. This tree is seen to be imbued with a continuing spiritual life-force that never sleeps. The pine therefore is also a symbol of longevity and continuity, reflecting Skuld's connection with the future.

Indigo

A blue approaching black that departs from the light-sourced colours of the rainbow bridge Bifrost.

Indigo is linked with the runes Wunjo (number 8), Hagalaz (number 9) and Nauthiz (number 10).

The solitary deity Hella, associated with the rune Hagalaz,

was set apart from the rest, as was her destiny – she reigned in gloom and isolation in the realm of Hel. This grim being is bounded on the one side by Wunjo with its image of joy and comfort, and on the other side by Nauthiz which indicates need and restraint.

Winter, with its dark indigo skies and bitter cold, was a time when many of the old and infirm died. It was these unfortunate souls who dwelt in Hella's world.

From here the colour order continues into the winter blackness of the sleeping earth.

There is only one tree association in this group and that is the beech, which is linked with Nauthiz. The beech tree symbolizes restraint, which is a theme of this particular rune.

Black

This colour denotes the complete absence of a light source in nature.

Black, the darkest colour, is created by mixing certain proportions of primary colours. Black's exact opposite, white, is produced in the form of light from the iridescent results of primary colours that are seen in a rainbow, or in a facet of crystal.

The progression of primary and secondary colours, as in the flaming rainbow bridge Bifrost, appeared to be a link between heaven and earth. However, the colours that would appear in the Web of Fate woven by the three Norns (Skuld, Urd and Verdandi), contained black, so black takes its allotted place in the order of the runes.

Black is associated with the runes Isa (number 11), Jera (number 12) and Eihwaz (number 13).

The associated deities in the same sequence as above are Skadi, Sif and Uller.

In Skadi we see the goddess of the cold black months and constant night of the Scandinavian winter.

Sif is the lovely goddess of the golden harvest. To achieve a successful harvest though, seeds must germinate and flourish in the black earth beneath the snows.

The presence of Uller the winter god was always indicated by the flashing lights of the Aurora Borealis against the black winter sky.

The alder and the yew are linked to Isa and Eihwaz (there is no tree association with Jera).

The common alder grows well by water and it is protected by water spirits, making it an important tree in folklore.

Water will form black ice on lakes in winter, so here we have the alder linked to the ice goddess Skadi. In snow-laden areas there could be dangerous depths of ice-covered water, a situation that could be fatal for the unwary traveller. The sight of an alder tree could prove a reliable warning of danger. One of the themes of the rune Isa is a warning of progress halted!

The yew was the god Uller's most favoured tree and he lived in a vale of yew trees which provided him with excellent wood for making hunting bows. The yew is traditionally a symbol of immortality and this tree has been recorded as having lived for two thousand years.

Green

This secondary colour is created by mixing the two primaries blue and yellow. In the order of runic colour significance, a green may also be made by mixing black with yellow.

Green represents the new shoots of plant life that emerge from the black soil. A successful harvest of corn and the growth of new vegetation was essential for man and animal alike, so green expresses the life-force, growth and fecundity.

Green is associated with Pertho (number 14), Algiz (number 15) and Sowulo (number 16). The deities Frigg, Heimdal and Baldur are associated with these runes, in the same sequence as above.

The goddess Frigg, the highest of the goddesses and the wife of Odin, epitomizes the perfect mother figure and one who is concerned with female fertility.

Heimdal, the 'watchman of the gods', was constantly on guard to protect the deities from harm, like a gardener looking after his sown seeds and new shoots.

Baldur the solar god expresses the sunlight that all plant life needs.

The three tree associations within this group are elm, lime and oak.

Elm and ash provided the wood from which the first male and female were made. The elm is capable of vigorous reproduction by sending out suckers to root and produce new saplings that gather about the mother tree, so the elm links with the mother image of Frigg. The elm leaf, in the language of flowers, says, 'Our love must remain a secret', again linking with the goddess Frigg who knew all things but remained silent.

The twigs that support the flowers of the lime tree are generally in formations of three and express the tri-form of the rune Algiz.

The oak is associated with Thor, whose righteous and aggressive energy made him brave and fearless. In the language of flowers, the oak, apart from its other associations, traditionally symbolizes morality, virtue and bravery. The oak also expresses Baldur's bravery when the sun god accepted his tragic destiny with dignity.

Yellow

This third primary colour is seen in the light of the sun. The yellow sun promotes growth and provides energy and warmth. The sun's yellow light allows clear vision. Yellow is also an expression of purity.

Yellow is linked with the runes Teiwaz (number 17), Berkana (number 18) and Ehwaz (number 19).

The deities linked with these runes, in the same sequence as above, are Týr, the Norn Urd and Iduna.

Týr had a wondrous golden sword which flashed with the yellow brilliance of the sunlight. His sword symbolized vitality, strength and divine truth.

Urd was one of the three Norns who directed the fates of men in their battle for survival down through the years. Yellow lent its attributes in the rainbow-coloured Web of Fate that she helped to weave in order to achieve this task.

Iduna, the goddess of eternal youth, kept apples in a gold casket. She distributed the apples to the gods and the fruit gave them vitality.

The tree associations within this group are hazel, birch and apple.

In reference to the hazel tree, the nut is traditionally thought to be a receptacle of supreme knowledge and the parent tree is linked with strength and protection. In these beliefs we can see the main attributes of the ancient god Týr. Yellow, the associated colour of Teiwaz, is to be seen in the colour of the seeds and male catkins of the hazel tree.

The birch, a tree that is venerated by witches and therefore linked to the goddess image, also has an association with yellow, which again can be seen in the colour of its seeds and male catkins.

The apple tree and its fruit have numerous traditional symbolic meanings that go far back in time, including the distribution of apples by Iduna the goddess of eternal youth. One of the most interesting associations that the apple has is with the Old Religion. If an apple is cut across the middle, the seed pattern that is revealed at the fruit's core is like a five-pointed star which in witchcraft is the pentagram. Witches therefore regard the apple as their sacred fruit.

Orange

This secondary colour links the primaries of yellow and red.

Orange is linked with the runes Mannaz (number 20), Laguz (number 21) and Inguz (number 22). The gods linked to the above runes (except Mannaz which is linked to man) are Njörd who is associated with Laguz, and Frey who is connected to Inguz.

Orange, like red, also represents fire and flames, and Njörd, the god of the seas and coastline, was also associated with flames. To quote the thirteenth-century Icelander Snorri Sturluson, 'He governs the movement of the winds and controls the sea and flame.'

Orange, like yellow, also represents a bountiful harvest. Frey, the god of sunlight, fruitfulness, peace and prosperity, would ride in his golden chariot with his sister Freya and distribute fruit and flowers to the waiting earth.

The solitary tree that is linked with this group is the willow, which is associated with Laguz.

The willow, whose young catkins have an orange hue, links with water which is the meaning of the rune Algiz.

From orange, the cycle flows back to red, the colour of Othila, of Dagaz and, completing the cycle, Fehu.

Gods and Goddesses

As legendary Norse gods and goddesses are a major feature of the Rune Vision Cards, it is appropriate to have a few words on the subject of deities.

The main gods and goddesses who figure in Nordic myth and legend often have several different names, and each name can have a number of different spellings according to the particular culture that recognizes the deity in question. Individual deities may also have responsibilities and attributes that often change during the passage of time.

If you find the world of gods and goddesses confusing then take comfort from the fact that a good many others are confused too! Help is at hand though.

Janet and Stewart Farrar, two well-known witches and writers, have compiled and written a couple of extensively researched works on the legendary deities. These companion volumes are *The Witches' God* and *The Witches' Goddess*. The Farrars have listed over two thousand gods and goddesses in their two reference works – and they have also included rituals for invoking individual deities. I highly recommend both volumes.

Appendix: The Author Talks to a Psychic

Jean Tighe has been working as a professional consultant for fifteen years. She has received wide media coverage and has also contributed to, and been mentioned in, books on occult subjects. Jean gives tarot, rune and astrology readings and is a counsellor. To contact Jean, see the Useful Addresses at the back of this book.

Howard Rodway: You have given me several very accurate readings over the years and on each occasion you have used a combination of the tarot and runes. Why do you use this system?

Jean Tighe: *The use of the tarot and runes in combination evolved naturally as I began giving readings. With the dual system I can gain a deeper insight and am able to give specific information to a client when this is necessary.*

HR: Most people know something about tarot cards but are less familiar with the runes. Do you find that your clients are a little in awe of these mystical symbols?

JT: *Yes, I believe you could say that, but this is mainly due to a lack of knowledge, and also misinformation. The tarot has frequently been dramatized on film and television. This is easy to do because of the visual impact of the tarot cards. The runes have a rich history too, but they are not easy to* *dramatize. Nevertheless, I feel more mysticism surrounds runes because through the ages there has been a strong tradition of passing on their meanings orally. Up until now the symbols have stood alone without embellishment.*

HR: Many of those who use the runes are witches. Do you feel that it is necessary to know something about our own native witchcraft tradition in order to appreciate the runes, which, in fact, also have a Celtic tradition?

JT: *No, I don't think it is necessary to know anything of the witchcraft tradition to appreciate the runes. The runes are used by wiccans and non-wiccans alike.*

HR: Would you recommend the runes for those who want to start giving readings but may find the tarot a little daunting to begin with?

JT: *I would thoroughly recommend the runes, especially for beginners. Some of my clients specifically ask for a rune reading alone, apprehensive of the appearance of certain tarot cards such as the Tower, Hanged Man or Death, perceiving them, often wrongly, as very negative indications. Runes don't seem to have quite the same negative associations, and for beginners they are simpler to work with and are more direct and to the point.*

HR: In this book I have given diagrams and explanations for three different card layouts to use. I always feel, though, that it is a good idea to experiment and create your own spreads.

Would you agree?

JT: *I agree one hundred per cent. Basic guidelines are of course needed, but then your own methods and spreads can be developed intuitively. On the other hand, I must also add that I see nothing wrong at all with sticking to a tried and tested layout if that is what works for you and you are entirely comfortable with it.*

HR: Do you have any additional tips or hints for reading the runes?

JT: *To be able to use any psychic tool well, a relationship has to be built up with it. Respect for and practice with your tool of choice are very necessary to achieve the best results.*

A good exercise is to select a rune sign each day and meditate upon it for a short period. Alternatively, choose a rune card or stone, and without looking at the symbol, place the card face down on your bedside table, or put the rune stone under your pillow before you go to bed. It is possible that you will dream of associations with that symbol. On waking you may also find that you intuitively know the symbol you have picked before looking at it. A good psychic knowledge of your tools helps you to give an in-depth reading.

HR: You have seen Sylvia's Rune Vision paintings. What do you think of her work?

JT: *Sylvia's artwork and artistic interpretation of the runic symbols are excellent, and her images certainly give a new and unusual dimension to the runes. I look forward to working with them.*

Bibliography

Farrar, Janet and Stewart, *The Witches' God*
(Robert Hale, London, 1995).

Pennick, Nigel, *The Complete Illustrated Guide to Runes*
(Element Books, Shaftesbury, 1999).

Rodway, Howard, *The Psychic Directory*
(Futura, London, 1984).

Rodway, Howard, *Tarot of the Old Path*
(Urania Verlags AG, Switzerland and US Games Systems,
USA. Several editions from 1990 onward).

Rodway, Howard, *Tarot of Northern Shadows*
(Urania Verlags AG, Switzerland, 1998).

Tracey, Kim, *Secrets of the Runes*
(Sphere, London, 1979).

Useful Addresses

Sylvia Gainsford
Gallery One
West Street
Fishguard
Pembrokeshire SA65 9AE
Wales
Tel: 01348 872707
49-page website:
www.abergwaun.com/
email: sylvia@abergwaun.com

Plant It 2000
PMB
9457 South University Boulevard
Highlands Ranch
Colorado 80126
USA
Tel: 303 221 0077
email: plantit@tesser.com
website: www.tesser.com/plantit/

Jean Tighe
7 Derwent Way
Rainham
Gillingham
Kent ME8 0BX
England
Tel: 01634 388648
Mobile: 07714 425300

The Woodland Trust
Autumn Park
Grantham
Lincolnshire NG31 6LL
England
Tel: 01476 581111

The Woodland Trust Northern Ireland
1 May Avenue
Bangor
County Down BT20 4JT
Northern Ireland
Tel: 01247 275787

The Woodland Trust Scotland
Glenruthven Mill
Abbey Road
Auchterarder
Perthshire PH3 1DP
Scotland
Tel: 01764 662554

A Quick Reference to
Meanings of the Rune Vision Cards

1 Fehu (p.19)
Divinatory significance:

Financial strength and prosperity is close. Love fulfilled. Desires nourished.

Reversed: Love thwarted. Disappointment. A Quarrel. Possible financial worries.

2 Uruz (p.23)
Divinatory significance:

Strength. Well-being. Support or news from afar. Be alert to an opportunity.

Reversed: Powers at a low ebb. A lost opportunity.

3 Thurisaz (p.27)
Divinatory significance:

Mischief making. Unreliability. A possible change. Do not act in haste because time will reveal a solution.

Reversed: A hasty decision causes anxiety and regret.

4 Ansuz (p.31)
Divinatory significance:

A visit, gift or advice from an older person. Learning wisdom.

Reversed: Interference from an older person. Duplicity.

5 Raido (p.35)
Divinatory significance:

A journey. Travel for relaxation and pleasure. A decision made to achieve an ambition. Career prospects. Communication.

Reversed: Arrangements hampered by a journey. Plans obstructed. A lack of direction.

 6 Kaunaz (p.39)
Divinatory significance:

For a woman, good fortune. A gift from a man.
For a man, pleasure from giving. Lust. Empathy. Enlightenment. The possibility of health problems. Physical or mental discomfort.

Reversed: Loss. Ending. Resignation. Facing the inevitable. Casting out the things of the past.

 7 Gebo (p.43)
Divinatory significance:

A good partnership or relationship. Love. Gifts bestowed.

Reversed*: Emotional problems. Disharmony.

 8 Wunjo (p.47)
Divinatory significance:

A blessing. Bliss. Devotion. Yearning. Be wary of pleasure in excess.

Reversed: Be wary in business matters. Impatience. Uncertainty. Strong impulse.

9 Hagalaz (p.53)
Divinatory significance:

Uncontrolled forces, either psychological or physical. A message concerning some disruption that is beyond control. Natural events could affect plans for the months or year ahead. Upsets. Risks.

Reversed*: Negativity. Beyond control.

 10 Nauthiz (p.57)
Divinatory significance:

Restrictions. Measured response. Plan carefully. The necessity to use restraint.

Reversed*: Unfortunate decision. Unsuitable behaviour or situation. Covetous or greedy attitude.

11 Isa (p.61)
Divinatory significance:

Taking a step backward. Withdrawn. Progress halted. A chill response. A parting. A lack of drive.

Reversed*: Infidelity. Treachery. (Isa reinforces those runes around it).

 12 Jera (p.65)
Divinatory significance:

A one-year period. Gaining what is rightfully yours. A professional person. Legal matters. Obligations. Harmony.

Reversed*: Taking a situation stage by stage. Completion cannot be rushed.

13 Eihwaz (p.69)
Divinatory significance:
A situation resolved. Conflicts can be overcome. Tenacity.

Reversed*: A lack of progress. The danger of defeat. Stress.

 14 Pertho (p.73)
Divinatory significance:
Fertility. Female concerns. Creativity. A surprise. Acquisition. A secret. A conundrum. Seductive. Discretion.

Reversed: High expectations can lead to dissatisfaction. Secrets betrayed.

 15 Algiz (p.77)
Divinatory significance:
A new position gained by effort or reward. A new job or pursuit will stimulate your intellect. A warning. Protection.

Reversed: Mislead. Beware of those who would take advantage of you. A weak position. Proceed with caution.

 16 Sowulo (p.81)
Divinatory significance:
Relax and rest. Take care of your health. Clarity. Clear vision. Achievement.

Reversed*: Egotistical. Self-centred.

17 Teiwaz (p.87)
Divinatory significance:

You know where your true strengths lie so make use of this knowledge. General success is indicated. A possible legal advantage. Honour. Leadership. A love-smitten man, if the enquirer is male. If the enquirer is female, great love will be hers.

Reversed: An untrustworthy relationship. Complications in romance.

18 Berkana (p.91)
Divinatory significance:

The family. A member of the family. Motherhood. News of a birth. Rebirth. Fertility.

Reversed: An upset with a member of the family. Family problems. Anxiety.

19 Ehwaz (p.95)
Divinatory significance:

A home change brings improvement. Progress. Reliability.

Reversed: Travel across water. Traumatic changes. Timing. When to act. (Ehwaz confirms those runes around it.)

20 Mannaz (p.99)
Divinatory significance:

Self. Reflection. Modesty. Humanitarian attitude. Delay signing any legal paper if you are undecided.

Reversed: Be warned of an enemy. The next rune will guide you on how to act. Selfish. Egotistical.

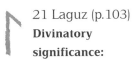 21 Laguz (p.103)
Divinatory significance:

Intuition. Psychic ability. Use your psychic insight. Acquisition. A successful pursuit. Birth.

Reversed: Work within your limitations.

 22 Inguz (p.107)
Divinatory significance:

Male fertility. Expectations for family, children and health. The completion of a project. A mental state is resolved.

Reversed*: Conclusions and beginnings. Stages of progress.

 23 Othila (p.111)
Divinatory significance:

Inheritance. Legacies. Spiritual heritage. Land. Property. Wills. Habitation. Fundamental values.

Reversed: Mechanical equipment may fail. Damage or an accident.

 24 Dagaz (p.115)
Divinatory significance:

Prosperity. Security. Growth. A change of situation for the better. A mental transition.

Reversed*: A traumatic change. A new perspective.

(If this rune is followed by
the blank rune it can mean
death or the end of a phase
to make way for a new one.)

25 Blank (p.119)
Divinatory significance:
Karma. Cause and effect.
Destiny. Fate. Inevitability.
Death. Ending.
Reversed:
None.